THEN AND THERE SERIES

GENERAL EDITOR

MARJORIE REEVES, M.A., Ph.D.

The
Medieval Tournament

*The Story of the Tournament at Smithfield
on 11th June, 1467*

R. J. MITCHELL

Illustrated from contemporary sources by

H. SCHWARZ

GW00992243

LONGMAN

LONGMAN GROUP LIMITED
London

Associated companies, branches and representatives
throughout the world

© R. J. Mitchell 1958

First published 1958
Eighth impression 1975

ISBN 0 582 20373 2

Printed in Hong Kong by
The Hong Kong Printing Press Ltd

Michele O'Rourke

CONTENTS

	Page
THE PROCLAMATION	1
PREPARING THE FIELD	6
THE ESQUIRES AND THE HERALDS	11
HERE COME THE SPECTATORS!	20
THE COMBAT	27
THE HAPPY ENDING	33
THE MEANING OF KNIGHTHOOD	35
HOW WE KNOW	40
THINGS TO DO	42
GLOSSARY	42

TO THE READER

DID you ever hear of a portrait 'drawn from life'? All the things described in this book are drawn from life, and the people as well. Nothing has been made up just for the sake of telling a story, everything happened exactly at the time and in the way that I have described. How do I know? Well, I found out by reading accounts written at the time, in chronicles, or official records, or in private letters, and those who were actually there at the time and who wrote down what they saw and heard are the best people to consult. They may have made mistakes in small things, just as you sometimes find misprints in books or newspapers, but I am showing you, as well as I possibly can, just how things seemed to the people who were there, and I would like you to feel that this is a book that you can really trust.

The pictures, too, are taken from those drawn at the time, and you can see some of them in museums or in libraries. These help you to imagine for yourselves what people looked like as well as how they felt. Perhaps it will surprise you to find that the people 'then and there'— though they looked rather different from ourselves— behaved in very much the same way as you and I would if we were dressed like that.

THE PROCLAMATION

IT WAS a very lucky thing that Thursday, 11th June, 1467, was a fine day, for if it had been wet and windy a very large number of people would have been disappointed.

The Town Crier of London had gone through all the streets ringing his bell and shouting at the top of his voice that the eleventh day of June was to be a public holiday, by the King's special order. There were no daily (or even weekly) newspapers to tell people of this treat, nor any radio, and it was not much good to write out and pin up a notice, for few people could read. So, when they heard his bell, everyone ran out of doors to listen to what the Town Crier had to say.

In some places, generally in very old towns that are not so important now as they were five hundred years ago, you can still hear the Town Crier ring his bell and 'cry' some announcement. This is not likely to be a holiday ordered by the Queen; you would probably hear that the water supply was going to be turned off, or that someone had dropped a brooch, or found a watch, or that a Youth Club dance was going to be held. None of these things, except perhaps the second, would have made sense to a townsman living in the fifteenth century, but the Town Crier was a very important person and everyone listened most carefully to what he had to say.

The reason for this extra holiday was soon explained. King Edward IV was married to a beautiful wife who loved to show off her jewels and rich clothes. Both she and King Edward enjoyed parties of all kinds, and the King wished also to show favour to his *ally*[1] the Duke of *Burgundy*. The excitement and colour and *pageantry* of a grand *tournament* would be just the thing to give pleasure all round, and so it was decided that the whole day of 11th June—and part of the next day—should be given up to this sport.

The Duke of Burgundy could not leave his own country just then, but his half-brother would come instead of the Duke and would himself fight with the King's own brother-in-law in the chief fight of the day. The name of both these knights was Anthony, so, to avoid muddle, we will describe them by their titles. The Englishman was Lord Scales and the other the Comte de la Roche.

You will want to know what sort of fighters these knights were, before you decide which of them you want to win. No doubt you will want to back the Englishman, but something happened during the fight that might make you change your mind. The Comte—we will write his name in English and call him the Count—was a very famous sportsman, skilful with both *lance* (on horseback) and with sword (on foot). He was noted not only for his politeness and his knowledge of all the rules of behaviour in these contests, but also for his generous conduct, whether he lost or won. We should call him a 'good sportsman'. Usually he won, and the Duke had made him a *Knight of the Golden Fleece*—the highest honour the Duke could give.

[1] You will find the meanings of words printed like *this* in the Glossary on page 42.

Lord Scales, too, had been honoured. The King had quite lately made him a *Knight of the Garter*. Here is a knight receiving the Garter in the presence of the King:

The Queen still gives this order to people who have served their country well. The Order has a very famous Latin motto which means "The shame be his who thinks ill of it". Do you think this is a good motto for a knight?

Lord Scales was several years younger than the Count and had not so much experience of real fighting. He was the kind of person who is very particular about his dress and the weapons he uses. This sort of thing seemed very important to Lord Scales, more important perhaps than the actual fighting. He was like a cricketer who takes three bats to the match with him, and lovely white pads, and then does not make many runs.

A tournament needed very careful planning. In this one the challenges to fight had been sent out long before the date was fixed. Several weeks before the Count was to arrive, orders had been given to collect the materials that would be needed and the labourers to do the work.

When the Count arrived on the last day of May, the *Lord Constable* of England went to meet him, with many lords and ladies and a host of London citizens, all in their best and brightest clothes. They rowed up the river Thames in *barges* decorated with bright hangings of blue and scarlet, and *awnings* laced with gold. The gay colours were reflected in the river, and the bands played lively music.

The Count's ship brought him up the Thames as far as Blackwall, and there the Londoners met him. There were greetings and speeches, and then the Count stepped on board one of the barges and the whole company turned about. With flags and streamers fluttering in the breeze and the sun shining on the brilliant colours, they came to Billingsgate. Here is the procession of barges sailing past the Tower of London:

At Billingsgate there were horses ready for them, with fine saddle-cloths and red leather bridles. The Constable rode with the Count to show him the rooms that had been prepared for him in Fleet Street. Here you can see some of the fine clothes that the lords and ladies wore for this special occasion:

The Bishop of Salisbury owned a grand house in Fleet Street that he had lent for the occasion. Even the bed-hangings were of cloth of gold, and food and wines and furniture were all of the very best that could be found. The Count stayed here several days and saw the sights of London—including the State Opening of Parliament by King Edward IV. He had never visited London before.

Lord Scales, too, was at the opening of Parliament, when he carried the Sword of State, but it was not correct for him to call and visit the Count before he had taken up the challenge. Now, at last, the great day of the tournament was at hand.

PREPARING THE FIELD

EVEN before the Town Crier had been sent out to make his proclamation, other people were hard at work preparing the ground where the tournament was to be. All sorts of things had to be considered before the field was chosen. First of all, the time of year. This would nearly always be in the summer. You know what a football ground is like after heavy winter rain, and you could not have horses and men in armour slipping about in mud.

The King had a number of palaces, shooting-lodges (for hunting), and manor houses in all parts of the country, but the most important tournaments were generally held in or close to London. At Eltham there was a famous ground where many exciting shows were held. For the greatest performances, however, when big crowds were expected, the large open space known as Smithfield was almost certain to be chosen, as it was in this year, 1467.

Smithfield, which means the 'smooth field' and not, as you may have thought, 'the field of smiths', had several advantages. There was enough space for the fighters to have plenty of room and for hundreds of spectators to have a good view, and extra ground behind the crowd for the *esquires* and *grooms*, the *harness* and the horses.

Smithfield had another advantage: it was so close to the city of London that it was easy for the crowds to assemble and to return home afterwards.

6

As the name tells us, it was a smooth field, with good grass and not too many bumps or hummocks. Even so, it had to be rolled and flattened as well as could be managed with a wooden roller, and any stones that had worked up to the surface had to be carried away. Stumbling against a stone might make a horse fall, and then his rider would come down too. This might make him lose the fight and he would certainly be very angry with the 'Steward of the Field', whose job it was to see that the ground was fit for a tournament.

In cold weather, and sometimes even in summer, the ground was covered thickly with straw for a day or two before it would be used. This is sometimes done to football grounds today, when frost is expected, but in the fifteenth century the straw was used more to keep it dry.

All through Wednesday, June 10th, until night fell, the groundsmen moved about their work. Carriers' carts came lumbering along, their wheels creaking, with loads of gravel to make the surface. Some of this gravel had to be brought from a distance, but the sand from the banks of the Thames was quite near at hand. The sand and the gravel were thumped and rolled into the ground, on top of the turf, until there was a really firm surface, gritty enough to stop the horses from sliding or falling when they were stopped quickly. Then came the dull thud of *mallets* striking wood, and the clang of hammers driving home iron nails, as the stands and the *barrier* were being set up.

Everyone knows what stands are; even today we are content to sit on wooden benches—only occasionally under cover—or huddle close together on the ground, to watch football or cricket. Nowadays, too, you have to pay extra money, just as you did in 1467, if you want a roof over your head or a cushion to sit on.

7

What was the purpose of the barrier when fighting in single *combat*? Each mounted knight had to stay on his own side of the canvas-and-wood barrier or division, looking like a fence, that ran from end to end of the pitch. In earlier times, before this barrier was invented, tournaments had been very rough and violent and a number of people and horses had been killed. Indeed, the fights had been forbidden by churchmen, and sometimes by the King as well, before the barrier made tournament-fighting safer and more skilful. This sketch may give you some idea of how the barriers and the stands were set up:

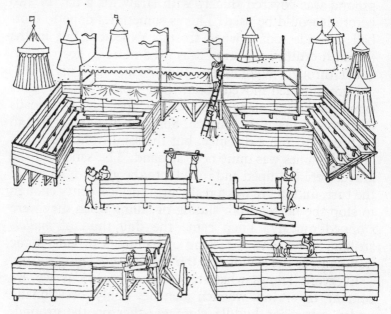

The barrier was easy to make—you could quite well make a model of one and stage fights between mounted knights cut out of plywood or cardboard and

8

suitably painted. It is rather fun to do, and you could stage this tournament of 1467, or any others that you happen to read about. At the time we are describing, canvas painted in bright colours was used, stretched on a wooden frame about four feet high. A few years later it would be made of solid wooden planks and raised to six feet high. This made the fighting, or *jousting*, safer but less exciting.

If you live near Worcester, you can go to the cathedral there and look for a tournament scene carved on the underside of one of the little wooden seats in the choir. If you live too far away you will have to make do with the picture of it drawn here for you:

Two knights are fighting fiercely. As this tournament took place before the barrier had been invented, the horses have collided and one of them is falling over backwards. The musician who was trying to amuse the onlookers has been knocked over and looks very much annoyed. I expect this made the crowd laugh a great deal.

Musicians, singers, and acrobats, though they did not as a rule find themselves mixed up with the fighters, were certainly on the ground. As soon as they heard the news that there would be a tournament at Smithfield, they would hurry to get there, and would begin to tune their instruments and rehearse their acts. The crowd might get impatient while waiting and be glad to spare a few half-pennies for some of these *minstrels* and *tumblers* who amused them during the pauses between the combats.

All these people were preparing for the great day, and at home mothers of families were planning meals and getting ready for the day's outing, but there were others even busier—those who had to see to the horses and the armour of the fighters. There were the *heralds*, too, and the stewards, and the Lord Constable who had to draw up the rules for the fighting: it is now time to look at the plans they, too, were making, for it is no good to have a perfect field if there is no one to sport upon it, and the sport itself is ruined if no one knows or keeps the rules.

THE ESQUIRES AND THE HERALDS

THE Lord Constable, who was a very careful man and very good at writing *ordinances*, or rules for special occasions, drew up a new set of rules specially made for this tournament. He would not trust such important work to his secretary, but really composed them himself, though they may have been written out by the secretary's hand.

This picture of the Lord Constable was drawn from his stone *effigy* in Ely Cathedral. His name was John Tiptoft, and he was earl of Worcester, so if you ever visit Ely, be sure to go into the cathedral to see him for yourself.

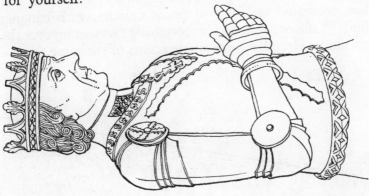

There is a copy of the rules for this tournament in the British Museum, and another at Oxford, so we are able to know exactly what the Constable said should happen. He said that if one fighter *unhorsed* the other by striking him to the ground he would win outright. If they both fell off the fight would be started again.

One thing the Constable made quite clear. The fighting was to be between the two men, and it would not be fair to try to bump or damage your opponent's horse so that he would fall or rear up and throw his rider. To make quite certain that everyone knew the rules, they were read in a loud voice by the herald just before the fight began.

The number of servants and pages and esquires that each knight might have to wait upon him was also laid down in the rules. A page was a young boy who was training to become an esquire, and the esquires were young men who were learning the rules of *chivalry*, and how to fight, and how to serve their masters. They hoped that they too would one day be knighted.

On either side of the tournament ground a large *pavilion* or tent had been set up for each knight and his esquires. It was decorated in his own special colours, with hanging folds of silk or satin, and his own badge was set up over the entrance. Here are some smaller tents of the same sort:

Many people think that these badges and *coats of arms* were just used as ornament and to show off a man's importance. You will, I believe, be more sensible than that. When a man's *visor* was down, how could you tell whether he was a friend or an enemy? His visor was the movable front of his helmet that protected his face, just leaving slits for seeing and breathing. Of course he had to wear something to show who he was, and that is how coats of arms began.

The son of a famous father naturally wanted to carry on with his pattern or *device*, and perhaps his mother also came from a great fighting family and he might wish to combine her family arms with his own. To show you how this worked, here is the coat of arms of this very Lord Constable who drew up the rules. His father had the family name of Tiptoft and his shield was decorated with a St. Andrew's cross, or *saltire*, in black with wavy edges, on a silver ground. His mother's shield carried a lion *rampant* in red on a golden ground. So here you can see his father's device on the left, his mother's in the middle, and his own, a combination of the first two, on the right:

The heralds, who had to know all about such matters, took care that no two families carried the same shield, and they had special names for the shapes and colours. If you like, you can describe the Constable's coat of arms quite correctly as: '*Quarterly*, 1 and 4 *argent* (silver) a saltire *engrailed*, *sable* (black); 2 and 3 *or* (gold) a lion rampant, *gules* (red).'

To make it even easier to tell friend from foe, many knights also wore a family badge and a *crest* fastened on to the top of their helmets. This did not always work out as it should. Let me tell you how the Yorkists won the battle of Barnet in 1471, during the Wars of the Roses. The day was misty, and in the heat of the battle the Lancastrians mistook Edward IV's badge of the 'sun with rays' for the Earl of Oxford's 'radiant star'. They discovered too late that they had joined the wrong side and so lost the battle. Servants, pages, and esquires, as well as men-at-arms, would all wear the family badge, but the crest was the knight's own special property, of which he was generally very proud. Here are some helmets with crests:

The crest was commonly made of wood; sometimes it was of leather boiled until it was quite hard and would no longer bend. It was a terrible weight to add to the already heavy helmet, and must have caused many headaches. It was placed over the knight's head after the rest of his armour had been fitted, for no-one could possibly wish to wear it for longer than was necessary. The helmet itself sometimes weighed as much as 20 lb.; it was padded inside so that it could stand up to bangs and blows like a modern crash-helmet. Here are helmets of different patterns:

In earlier days knights had worn *chain-mail* made of small metal rings, and in this it was far easier to move about than in the *plate* armour worn in the fifteenth century. It is true that the large pieces of metal, jointed at hip, knee, wrist, and elbow, and with special shields for the jointed shoulder, did give better protection against heavy blows and perhaps saved the wearer from bruises, but it must have been very uncomfortable to wear.

As to the weight—have you ever tried to lift half a hundredweight of potatoes? That is 56 lb., and the ordinary armour of a knight at this time, not counting his helmet, shield, or lance, worked out at nearer 60 lb.! These knights have put on all their armour except for the helmets, which they will put on just before they mount their horses. Do you see the special pieces which cover their shoulders and elbows?

Shields were not quite so heavy in the year 1467 as they would have been in the earlier days of chain mail. The stronger the armour, the less need for an enormous shield. It would be very awkward and clumsy to have too large a shield, and there was much to be said for the neat, nearly square ones that had a notch at the side to make a rest for one's lance.

Let us watch Lord Scales being dressed in his own tent by his favourite esquire and pages. His suit of armour might have looked like this one. He is already wearing a rough cloth shirt made from stuff known as *fustian*, but as he has a tender skin he has had it lined with satin. There is a padded collar and the shoulders are thickly covered with woollen padding to keep the edges of the armour from rubbing him. For the same reason he has on a pair of long and very thick woollen stockings.

As Lord Scales sits down on a three-legged stool and the pages begin to fasten on the leg-pieces of his armour, we see that there are many stiff pieces of leather sewn on to his shirt and *hose*. Some are pierced with eyelet holes, and we guess that the different pieces of armour will be fastened on to them. For, by now, we have given up the idea that to get inside a suit of armour you had to jump in from the top or wriggle up from the bottom.

When you see suits of armour standing in museums, at the Wallace Collection or the Tower Armoury in London for instance, it is at first difficult to imagine that everything can be taken to pieces. When you look closely, however, you see that there are many fastenings, mostly buckles, or laces and rivets, and once they have been put in the right order they are quite easy to fix.

Some knights also wore leather clothes under their mail, but these added to the weight and were almost unbearably hot. Men living in those days were on the whole rather smaller than they are today, so the small suits of armour that we see probably fitted very well. They were made to measure and according to the wearer's wishes. You would not go to the armourer's shop and say "I want a standard suit of plate armour to fit chest size 38." The armourer himself would call upon you, with two or three of his men to help measure you. You might say: "Make me a suit of armour like the one Lord Scales wore in his last fight, but remember that I am much larger in the arms. And I won't have any hooks or rivets sticking into me; if you have to make extra fastenings, they are all to be straps made from the softest possible leather."

Now all the pieces of plate have been fastened in position, and Lord Scales is ready to mount his horse. Here is the page bringing the helmet. This must be held above his head and gently brought down to rest on those padded shoulder-pieces. Then he will have to be helped into the saddle, for only a very strong and athletic man could *vault* there from the ground. Pull on his *gauntlet gloves*, bring him his shield and his lance, and he will be ready to fight.

All this time, the grooms have been getting ready the horse that Lord Scales is to ride. It is a big fellow, rather like a farm-horse of today, perhaps a Suffolk Punch. It is not fast, but it is very, very strong, and trained to carry the great weight of its master and its own armour besides. For the horse is protected as well as the knight, especially about the head and neck. Here is the horse ready for Lord Scales to ride:

The saddle is huge and high and heavy too. It is shaped rather like a chair, with high pieces fore and aft to help the rider keep his seat. *Stirrups* are more for ornament than for use. Embroidered saddle-cloths, and decorations called *trappings*, with huge reins of *scalloped* leather, often trimmed with gold, all look very grand but make the horse's task a hard one.

It is not surprising that when horse and rider fall, neither can get up without help, and far more knights die from suffocation by the weight of their own armour than are ever killed in battle. Armour can turn away blows from sword or lance, but it can also be very dangerous to its wearer.

19

HERE COME THE SPECTATORS!

EVERYONE wanting a good view took care to get along to Smithfield early in the morning. You know that there are all-night queues to watch the tennis finals at Wimbledon, and that people travel all night from distant parts to be in time for the Cup Final. Well, everyone who could possibly manage it wanted to be in the front row at Smithfield so that he could see just what happened, and feel a spice of danger himself. Horses might plunge and rear, carelessly aimed lances could snap and the pieces fly through the air and fall close to the spectators. There was always just the chance that your neighbours, and even you yourself, might be caught up in the fight. Do you remember what happened to the musician in the picture on page 9? If you felt you would rather watch from a safe distance you could sit well back on the stands.

The front row of spectators started by sitting on the ground but jumped to their feet when things became exciting. Some brought three-legged stools, and when they stood on these to see better, there were loud cries of "Sit down!" just as there would be today. Probably they were louder, for crowds were rougher then, and not much used to being shown where to go and what to do. Sometimes there were fights, and people would get hurt. Some people brought skin cushions stuffed with hair or moss, for the ground was hard when you sat on it for several hours. Only rather rich people had cushions, and those who brought them to the tournament were thought to be showing off.

The people who had started early in the morning soon became hungry and thirsty. Some would have brought food with them, packed overnight and by now rather dull and dry. Others bought from the sellers of hot pies, who had brought charcoal *braziers* with them and were cooking meat pies upon the field. They did a good trade, and it was a temptation to re-heat pies made the day before and sell them as fresh, although this was strictly against the rules of the Cooks' *Gild*. Wine, or sometimes water, was carried in skins, and those who had forgotten to bring cups or flasks of their own could put their mouths to the skin and drink all they could in one draught, at the cost of a few pence. This pleased the thirsty, and saved the trouble of providing drinking cups, but it was a sure way of spreading infection. Perhaps this is one of the reasons why disease spread so far and so fast in those days.

As it was a public holiday, all the London *apprentices* were there, in a very merry mood. Here is a stand crowded with eager spectators:

They yelled and laughed and sang, happy to be free from their masters for a whole day, for they were kept hard at work learning their trade, and even when work was finished they had to wait upon their master and his family. Good masters taught them also to read and write, but not many of them thought their apprentices needed time for play. If the apprentice was stupid or lazy he would certainly be beaten, and even if he tried his best and did really well, there were times when he simply had to break out and make a wild noise. So you can see how miserable the apprentices would have been if the rain had come down in torrents and the tournament had had to be cancelled.

Of course all the masters and their families, and all the labourers of London were there. Now the lords and ladies, knights and esquires and all the more important people were beginning to arrive. In fact, every kind of person you can think of was eager to watch the tournament, and every single one of them was determined to enjoy himself.

Here are some London craftsmen with their tools. But of course they would not have their tools with them on this day!

The long time of waiting passed quickly enough with everyone in a good holiday temper, ready to laugh at jokes and to tell each other stories. Old men were glad if anyone would listen to their long tales of tournaments they had seen when they were young. Knowledgeable young men shook their heads wisely and knew exactly what was going to happen. The merchants' wives talked to each other about the royal family. News and gossip spread through the crowd, each person adding a little to what he had heard. In fact, they behaved very much as any crowd has behaved from the people who watched the wild-beast shows at Rome to those who come flocking to the Derby today. They had come to enjoy themselves, and enjoy themselves they would.

The only real difference was in the brightness of colour. Partly because the number of people there was very small indeed compared with today's crowds, the colours looked far brighter and it was easy to pick out one's own friends. Everyone wore coloured clothes, both men and women, and although poorer people were not supposed to wear rich and gorgeous clothes and might be fined if they did so, they were all dressed in the best things that they had.

The crowds, waiting as patiently as they were able, knew that they could expect an exciting fight, and kept shouting that it was time to begin. "Come on out," they said, "it is time to leave your pavilions and give us something to watch." The *Flemish* merchants and craftsmen who lived in London had all come out to see their countryman, half brother to their own Duke and very popular in his own land. They shouted, too, in their own language.

Those of you who are smart at spotting mistakes will be saying: "There's something wrong here. The Count's

23

half-brother was the Duke of Burgundy, not of *Flanders*, where these *Flemings* came from!" There is a reason, though, and here it is. The Duke of Burgundy was also Count of Flanders! He held lands that very nearly made a middle state between France and Germany and he may have had the idea of forming a great central kingdom from these rich lands. So you can see how it was that the English king was anxious to have this duke for a friend, and why he wanted to do honour to his brother.

Late-comers who could not squeeze into the enclosure had to climb trees if they wanted to look over the heads of the spectators already on the ground. From here they could see the royal party riding towards Smithfield long before those below had any idea they were in sight. There was a stir when the Lord Mayor and aldermen of the City of London arrived, and made their way into the special stand that had been put up for them, opposite the royal box.

Suddenly, a whisper ran round the ground: "Here are the umpires," as the splendid figures of the Earl Marshal and the Lord Constable were seen, standing in front of the royal box. "The King must be coming," said some-one, and a murmur ran through the crowd: "The King is coming, the King is coming!"

The three *tiers of seats* below the royal box had filled up long ago. Here were the knights and esquires and their ladies, all of them dressed with great magnificence. After the tournament was over, one of the Knights who was in attendance on the Earl Marshal sent to his master a bill for 300 marks. (What would that mean in today's money? Try multiplying by 35, and your answer should come out in pounds sterling.) He said this was what the show had cost him.

A great flourish of trumpets, and loud and loyal cries from those standing near the entrance, announced that the King and Queen had come, with their special friends and all the King's councillors except the two who were to act as umpires. The King looked splendid: a Frenchman who saw him afterwards wrote in his *Chronicle*: "This must be the handsomest man in Europe!" King Edward IV was very tall and rather fair and fresh-coloured, with a smiling face, and he was very popular with the Londoners. On this day he was wearing a purple robe and those near to him could see that he had the Order of the Garter at his knee.

Of course everyone stood up when the King arrived. Now, they were all sitting down again, and first Lord Scales and then the Count rode up to the royal box to ask for permission to begin. Here are the King and Queen in the royal box:

Both the champions then went back to their tents to finish arming and to put on their helmets, and at the four corners of the field four heralds together read their proclamations.

The spectators were warned not to make any noise or movement that might upset the fighters or their horses, and to keep back their cheers and shouting until the round was over. The rules of the tournament were read out, just as the Constable had drawn them up, so that there could be no mistake, and at last the heralds withdrew. The blue satin tent belonging to Lord Scales opened suddenly, and at the other side of the ground the Count's tent also. Both the champions appeared, mounted their horses, and sat upright, waiting for the heralds' cry of "*Laissez aller*." The fight had begun.

THE COMBAT

THE AIM of every knight fighting in a tournament was to knock his opponent off his horse, at the first possible chance, with a violent body blow from his lance. The best way of getting real power behind this blow was to deliver it when the horse was moving at his fastest speed, so horse and rider acted together. The horses, then, were trained to break at once into a slow canter which was the best speed that they could manage, weighed down as they were with their own armour, the silk trappings, and the great weight of their riders.

Starting at the same time from opposite points, the knights were likely to meet in the middle of the barrier, that is, half way across the field. As everyone expected, that is what happened, but no one on the ground, or in the boxes, expected to see what happened next. Both the champions seemed to have missed their mark, there was a scuffle, then a snort and a scream from the Count's horse. It reared high into the air and then fell to the ground and lay still—dead!

For a second there was silence, and then everyone began to shout. Only a few minutes earlier they had heard the rule read out: "He that *smiteth* his opponent's horse shall have no prize." Some people thought the Count's horse had collided with the barrier, that there had been an accident. Lord Scales exclaimed that he had not struck the horse. The Count, who had fallen heavily with his horse, was being picked up by his esquires: he had taken off his helmet and everyone could see his red and furious face.

27

Only the Lord Constable knew what to do. Lord Scales was rich and powerful, he was brother-in-law to the King, there was sure to be trouble if he were disqualified; but this umpire knew that he was there to see that the rules were kept, rules that he had himself drawn up. He went straight up to Lord Scales and made him dismount. Then, with his own hands he tore away the trappings from the saddle and showed that under the silk cloth was a great heavy piece of metal clamped on to the saddle, with a spike that could kill a horse if it were to strike it above the height of the barrier—as, indeed, it had. When asked to explain why it was there, Lord Scales stammered that it was a special design of his own to make his saddle more comfortable and was never meant to hurt his opponent's horse. It was all a mistake, a pure accident, he said.

The Lord Constable looked at him with contempt. He would not even allow Lord Scales to appeal to the King. "You are disqualified," he said shortly. "It was a foul blow." And he awarded the fight to the Count.

Matters looked very awkward. The King, who was himself a good sportsman, was deeply shocked by his brother-in-law's behaviour, but after a time he, and others, began to wonder if it really had been an accident. Lord Scales was very distressed and declared he had never meant to strike a foul blow. He begged the Count to take another horse and go on with the fight, but this the Count was not willing to do, although he had now recovered his temper.

The Earl Marshal, the other umpire, said it was not his business to interpret the rules, and to give advice about matters of chivalry, while the Lord Constable looked grimmer than ever, and people began to remember that he was a stern man and not popular in the country. The Queen's father, Lord Rivers, said there was a lot of fuss about very little, and advised the King to cancel the fight on horseback and to let the Count and Lord Scales fight it out on foot. This the Count agreed to do, but not until the next day.

There were other fights that same day but nothing else so unexpected happened. In this fight, for example, there is no suspicion of foul play. Which of the knights will win, do you think?

All the people were pleased at the prospect of a second holiday, and went home talking hard over this very unusual happening. One of them, a very sharp and sensible man, wrote in his chronicle that night: "I know not what I shall say of it, whether it was fortune, craft, or cunning." What do you think? I feel like William Gregory who wrote the chronicle, for if Lord Scales 'arranged' the accident on purpose, how could he hope it would pass unnoticed? On the other hand, that piece of metal specially attached to his saddle does take a lot of explaining.

What discussion there was that night round every supper-table in London! Some were for Lord Scales, some were against him, but everyone agreed that the fight next day was bound to be very exciting. The Londoners were off early the next morning to get good places, for no one wanted to miss seeing this second fight. Soon they were all packed tightly together and everyone was waiting breathlessly when the champions came forth.

There was little waiting about at this second meeting between the knights. Both were grimly anxious to fight, the Count to avenge the insult to his honour, Lord Scales to show that he was a real fighter and did not have to use a trick to defeat his opponent. From the first clash of arms it was clear that there would be no easy *thrust* and *parry*, but real and savage blows.

The weapons chosen were axes and daggers, in place of the more usual swords. This meant close fighting at short range. The Lord Constable was determined that there should be no more trouble and had made careful arrangements for recording in writing every hit scored. Two special heralds had been appointed for each side, and there they were with pens, ink, and papers: one to watch and the other to write down every time one of the fighters hit his opponent. These officials stood on either side of the royal box, and there were heralds too in the royal box to tell the King how the fight was going.

Lord Scales sprang from his pavilion crying, "St. George! St. George! St. George!" and he and the Count set about each other at once with their axes. These had heavy heads and long handles and when they clashed against the armour after a full swing the din echoed all round the field. The spectators were absolutely quiet; only the heralds shouting the score and the heavy breathing of the fighters could be heard in the intervals between the blows.

Soon, the armour of both men showed dents and gashes from the blows, but neither would give up. It looked as though the fight would end in the death of one or both of the knights.

Suddenly, King Edward IV rose up in his seat and threw down the *baton* he carried, dropping it between the knights as a signal that the fight must stop. The Count and Lord Scales rested on their axes for a moment, regaining their breath, and then at the King's order, shook hands to show that their fight was over.

Again, as on the day before, opinion was divided. On one thing, however, all were agreed. It had been a great fight, both knights had shown great skill and courage, and there was little to choose between them.

The Londoner, William Gregory, who was present at both fights and had not been able to make up his mind about the 'foul blow', said of this one: "they fought on foot full well." Gregory did not like to name the winner where both had done so well, and he summed up what most people thought when he wrote in his chronicle—"ask of them that made the blows, they can tell you best."

THE HAPPY ENDING

IT IS not often that a story comes to an end with something good happening for everybody. When it does, we are likely to say "what a fairy-story!" The thing about this story, though, is that it is absolutely true.

Certainly it was the right ending for the tournament, for in watching the very spirited axe-and-dagger fight on foot everyone forgot the trouble of the day before. The crowd had seen something really worth watching and had enjoyed one of the finest tournaments ever staged at Smithfield. The other fights were good ones too, and worthy of the grand prizes that were given.

Later on the Count and Lord Scales met again at a tournament. It was held at Bruges, in the Low Countries across the sea. The market-place was completely cleared, stalls swept away into side-streets, and the paving-stones and *cobbles* thickly scattered with gravel. This time our two heroes met as friends, not enemies, for soon after the Smithfield tournament they had made a pledge that they would never fight each other again, and the hand-shaking ordered by the King became a sign of real friendship.

The reason for the Bruges tournament, and the pageants that went with it, was the marriage of Duke Charles 'the Bold' (or, some said, 'the Rash') of Burgundy to King Edward's sister, Margaret. This marked an alliance that King Edward and his advisers had wanted for a long time, and the earlier tournament had been just one step in this direction. There were *banquets*, and plays, and music and dancing; the celebrations went on for several weeks and cost a great deal of money.

We said that something good for everybody came out of the happenings at Smithfield, but we have forgotten one person, as well as the poor horse that was killed by the spike on Lord Scales' saddle. This person was the Lord Constable, who felt sour and angry that the King had favoured Lord Scales after the umpire himself had disqualified him. The Queen and Lord Rivers had not been pleased by the Constable's harsh words, and they persuaded the King to send him away to Ireland, to be the King's *Deputy* and to try to keep order there. Many people—though not the Irish—were glad to hear that the Constable was leaving England, for he was a harsh and stern man and not much liked by the common people, although he could be charming to his friends.

The tournament at Smithfield had come at a time when Londoners wanted a break. It had given them excitement and pleasure, and, above all, it had provided everyone with a very delightful holiday.

THE MEANING OF KNIGHTHOOD

Now, what was this tournament all about? I will tell you. It was a 'knightly exercise'. Knighthood was a very serious business. Now and again a young man might still be knighted on the battlefield, if he had done something outstandingly brave or brilliant that happened to catch the eye of the King, but this was becoming rarer as the years passed by. At the time we are describing, the middle years of the fifteenth century, there was generally a long and careful preparation leading up to the great day when the young man to be knighted would kneel bareheaded before the throne.

Part of the preparation was called the *vigil*. The young man had already been taught the rules of knightly behaviour, and he was left to spend the whole night before the great day dawned, kneeling in prayer before God's altar. Alone and in the dark, in the silence of the night, the high ideals must have seemed very solemn, as he prayed that he might truly fulfil the *vows* he would take next day. His arms and weapons lay in front of him, and when the light of day came faintly through the church windows, two other knights came for him and he went to make his confession and hear Mass.

After a few hours' rest, for the vigil had been very tiring, the young man was dressed in special garments for his knighthood. These were: a white tunic, a red robe, and a black doublet, which stood for his innocence, self-sacrifice, and death.

Two of the oldest and noblest knights then fastened his *spurs* and *girded on* his sword. Saying to him "Be thou a good knight", they led him to the King. Taking his sword in his hand, the King would strike him lightly on the shoulder—not with the edge, but with the flat—and say "Arise, Sir John!" (or "Sir Richard", or "Sir Robert", or "Sir Anthony"). Here is the King about to knight the kneeling man. A courtier holds the King's sword ready:

This was a great moment and a great honour to be taken very seriously. Not only would the new knight have the honours of his rank, there were also many things he must undertake to do and be.

It was a knight's duty to be gentle and *courteous* always, not only towards those of his own rank and those above him, but to lesser people as well. He must never, never, never be proud of his rank but must accept his duties humbly and do his very best to carry them out. Above all, it was his duty to protect the weak, old people, and children, and to honour women.

He must serve the King faithfully and bravely, without grumbling or complaint. He must fear God and protect his religion, he must speak the truth and avoid all mean-ness and deceit. A true knight showed mercy to a defeated enemy, but he would never forgive an insult to himself or to anyone under his protection. Nor would he ever refuse a challenge to fight, if it came to him from someone of equal rank, and never, either in tournament or in battle, would he give up and turn his back upon a foe.

The young knight wore on his left shoulder a *lace*, or white silk cord doubled in half, sewn on to his cloak. This he would have to wear until he had won some great renown or honour, fighting bravely and skilfully perhaps in some important tournament, or in a real battle. The King himself, or some great noble, would cut away the lace, and then the young knight would know that he had passed the test and that he was accepted into the order of chivalry.

Sometimes, at a tournament, the lace would be cut away by some noble lady, even the Queen herself. It was the custom for every knight, both old and young, to carry with him some small *emblem* of the lady whose praise he hoped to win. It might be a glove, or possibly a flower that she had given him. You know how an actor sometimes plays his part for one special person in the audience, thinking of this one person and speaking directly to them? You have probably done it yourself, or when you are playing games you like to feel there is one person whose praise and admiration you specially want. This is very natural and it is the same sort of feeling that knights had when they were fighting for some lady and carried her emblem to remind them that they must do their best. It did not matter whether other people knew or not whose was the emblem; it could be quite a private matter. But many knights said openly whose emblem they wore, especially if it belonged to the Queen. Here is a knight kneeling before his lady:

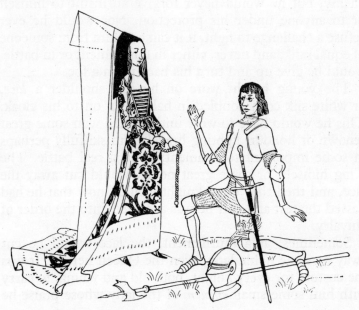

A knight who fought in tournaments only to win prizes, and to beat his opponent by any means he could, would not win much praise or much respect. Crowds then, as now, liked to see generous and gallant behaviour. They cheered loudest for the man who would not take advantage of someone disabled by accident, and who was modest when he did win a fight. This, together with real courage in facing heavy odds, made up the chivalry that was so greatly admired and must be shown by anyone worthy of knighthood.

It was easier to carry out these ideas in tournaments than on the actual battlefield, but true knights always remembered the rules of chivalry even when fighting for their lives. The tournaments were, in fact, very useful training for real war. They kept men and horses in condition and gave them the practice they needed in handling heavy weapons.

This is what one very sensible man thought about tournaments. The words are his, though the spelling has been changed. The writer was William Caxton, the first printer to set up his press in England. "Oh you knights," he said, "what do you (now) but sleep and take your ease?" He wished the King would order tournaments two or three times a year, so that "every knight should have horses and harness and the craft of a knight, the best to have as prize a diamond or (other) jewel. This should cause gentlemen always to be ready to serve their prince when he shall call them or have need."

HOW WE KNOW

WE know all about this great tournament, and many others, because they were written about in chronicles. We know that everything happened exactly as I have told you because the chronicler wrote down what he actually saw.

Another famous chronicler, whose name was Sir John Froissart, described in his chronicles the tournaments that he watched. Here is the description, in Froissart's own words, of one which was held at Smithfield to entertain some French visitors. This tournament took place 77 years before the one I have been describing; in what ways were they similar?

The King ordered grand tournaments and feasts to be held in the city of London, where sixty knights should be accompanied by sixty noble ladies richly ornamented and dressed. The sixty knights were to *tilt* for two days; that is to say, on the Sunday after Michaelmas day, and the Monday following, in the year of grace 1390. They were to set out at two o'clock in the afternoon from the Tower of London with their ladies, and parade through the streets, down Cheapside, to a large square called Smithfield. There they were to wait on the Sunday the arrival of any foreign knights who might want to joust.

The same ceremonies were to take place on the Monday, and the sixty knights were to be prepared for tilting courteously, with blunted lances. The prize for the best knight of the opponents was a rich crown of gold, that for the home side a very rich golden clasp. They were given to the most gallant tilter, according to the judgement of the ladies who should be present with the Queen of England, and the great lords. On Tuesday the tournaments were to be continued by squires against others of the same rank who wished to oppose them. The prize for the opponents was a war horse saddled and bridled, and for the home side a falcon.

So on Sunday afternoon there paraded from the Tower of London sixty splendid horses ornamented for the tournament, and on each was mounted a squire of honour. Then rode sixty noble ladies most elegantly and richly dressed, each leading a knight with a silver chain, completely armed for tilting; and in this procession they moved through the streets of London to Smithfield, attended by many trumpets and minstrels.

When the tournament began everyone fought as hard as possible, many were unhorsed and many more lost their helmets. The jousting continued with great courage until night put an end to it. At suppertime the prize for the opponents at the tournament was given by ladies, lords and heralds to the Count d'Ostrevant, who far excelled all who had tilted that day.

On the Tuesday, the tournament was renewed by the squires, who tilted until night in the presence of the King, Queen and nobles. The supper was as before at the bishop's palace, and the dancing lasted until daybreak. The remainder of the week was spent in feasting, and the King conferred the Order of the Garter on Count d'Ostrevant—which annoyed many of the French visitors.

THINGS TO DO

1. Make a model of the tournament at Smithfield out of cardboard or plywood.

2. Write an account of the tournament as if you were a London citizen who watched it all from the front row and then went home and put it in his diary.

3. Go to a museum where there are suits of armour and make a drawing to show the different pieces of armour. If there is no museum near, get a book about armour from the library and make your drawings from this. If you can, put the date of each piece by your drawing and notice whether it is earlier or later than the Smithfield tournament.

4. Collect as many family coats of arms and crests as you can. Draw and paint them in the proper colours and, if you can, find the right words to describe them.

GLOSSARY

This is a list of special words. If the word you want to know is not here, look for it in your dictionary.

ally: friend.
apprentice: boy or young man learning a trade.
argent: heraldic term meaning silver.
awning: roof of canvas or cloth to give shelter.
banquet: feast.
barge: large, flat-bottomed boat.
barrier: fence across the middle of the *tournament* ground.
baton: short stick.
brazier: iron basket in which fire burns.
Burgundy: formerly a middle state between France and Germany.
chain-mail: armour made of little iron rings linked together.
chivalry: rules of good behaviour for knights.
chronicle: history of events.

coat of arms: special badge belonging to a family.
cobbles: small round stones used to pave a street.
combat: fight.
courteous: polite.
crest: badge worn on top of a helmet.
deputy: someone who takes the place of another person.
device: badge.
effigy: likeness of a person usually carved in stone.
emblem: badge.
engrailed: heraldic term to describe a cross on a shield when it has a wavy edge.
esquire: young man learning to be a knight.
Flanders: land we now call Belgium.
Flemings: people who lived in *Flanders*.
Flemish: from *Flanders*.
fustian: rough stuff for clothes.
gauntlet gloves: leather gloves with long pieces up the arms.
gild: company of merchants of a particular trade.
to gird on: to buckle round the waist.
groom: man who looks after horses.
gules: heraldic term meaning red.
harness: leather trappings for a horse.
herald: king's messenger who goes in front of the king or makes royal announcements. The herald also knows all about *coats of arms* and *crests* and other heraldic *devices*.
hose: long stockings.
joust: mock fight.
Knight of the Garter: knight belonging to an order with a garter for a badge.
Knight of the Golden Fleece: knight belonging to an order with a golden fleece (i.e. sheep's wool) for badge.
lace: silk cord worn by a young knight on his left shoulder.
laissez aller: French words meaning 'Off!'. They were used to start a tournament.
lance: spear.

Lord Constable: one of the King's most important officials.

mallet: heavy hammer.

minstrels: musicians.

or: heraldic term meaning gold.

ordinances: rules for special occasions.

pageantry: wonderful and colourful show.

to parry: to turn aside a sword *thrust.*

pavilion: large tent.

plate: describing armour made of solid pieces of metal.

quarterly: heraldic term to describe a shield whose device is divided into four equal parts.

rampant: heraldic term to describe an animal standing on its hind legs.

sable: heraldic term meaning black.

saltire: heraldic term meaning a cross shaped like the letter X.

scalloped leather: leather cut with a wavy edge.

to smite: to hit hard.

spurs: sharp iron points worn by a rider on his heels to prick the horse and make it go faster.

stirrups: rests for the rider's feet hung on either side of a horse.

thrust: hit.

tiers of seats: seats in rows one above the other.

tilt: charge with lance.

tournament: mock battle.

trappings: harness for a horse.

tumbler: acrobat.

to unhorse: to knock someone off his horse.

vault: jump.

vigil: all night watch.

visor: movable front of a helmet to protect the face.

vow: solemn promise.